RHYTHM AND MOVEMENT

Can · Make · and · Do Books

RHYTHM AND MOVEMENT

160 Experiences for Children, Including Patterns to Use with Sticks, Cups, Balls, Rags, Hoops and Rope

by Joy Wilt
Terre Watson

Photography by John Hurn
Terry Staus
Jack Woodward

CREATIVE RESOURCES
Waco, Texas

Acknowledgment

Some very special friends have contributed their expertise, enthusiasm and time to produce this book. Five of these friends have special talents which they have graciously shared with us. Julie Escarsega, our editor—thank you for taking the time from your busy schedule to edit this book. Melena Edmonston—thank you for your time spent in editing and typing. John Hurn, Terry Staus, and Jack Woodward, our photographers—thanks for your skill and knowledge.

There are some very special children we would love to thank for their patience, enthusiasm and self-discipline in sitting through the photography sessions. Thank you to Troy Berry, Amber Call, Tom and Gena Finlay, Shelby and Marty Free, Marie Hewett, Joel and Leah Hunter, Mandy Keegan, Kathleen and Ken Kotchnik, Lorri McBrayer, Allison and Christine Persing, Carina Scott, Meagan Silva, Mitzi and Matt Watson, Lisa and Christopher Wilt, and Lanny Zamora.

JOY WILT
TERRE WATSON

Contents

Introduction

This book describes sounds and movements that can be executed with or without a partner. In addition, there are movements and patterns to be done with sticks, cups, hoops, rags, balls, and ropes.

The individual movements employ one of two kinds of rhythmic activity: making sounds with the mouth or other parts of the body, or performing a movement that takes up a beat without making a sound. By combining the two, rhythm patterns can be created for songs or anything else of 4/4 or 3/4 time.

Each chapter explains individual movements first and then combines them in patterns. Try them; then as you become familiar with these sound rhythms and body pass movements, make up your own patterns or have the children create patterns together.

For the sections on sticks, cups, hoops, balls, rags, and ropes, you will need the following: ¾″ x 12″ wooden dowels; 1-cup metal measuring cups; 8″ or 10″ inflatable rubber bounce balls; ¾″ Hula Hoops (by Wham-O); ¾″ ropes in 6′, 10′, and 16′ lengths. Terry cloth or cheesecloth dish towels, pieces of old sheets or other material are suitable for rag rhythms. Each activity lists separately the number of items needed.

No specific songs or words to go with the patterns have been suggested here because you can use any song, poem, verse, or rhyme you want to recite. Add rhythms and body movement to your activity—interest, enthusiasm, and participation will increase. Have fun creating!

Mouth Sounds and Body Sounds

Mouth Sounds

The mouth and tongue are capable of producing many varied noises which can be used for rhythm sounds. These sounds are made by varying the position of the lips, teeth, tongue, and the amount and direction of the air being taken in or out of the mouth.

1. To make a **squish** sound, take a deep breath and hold the air in your cheeks. With your hands, gently tap your cheeks to force the air out of your mouth.
2. Prepare for the **click** sound by placing the tip of your tongue against the lower front teeth while the mouth is open and smiling. Make the clicking noise with the back of the tongue.
3. To produce the **cluck** sound, place the tip of the tongue on the roof of the mouth; then bring it down to strike the bottom of the mouth.
4. For the **chug** sound, begin with the lips open, teeth together, and the tip of the tongue against the upper front teeth. Blow air out of the mouth as you pull the tongue down to the lower half of the mouth and open the teeth.
5. For the s-s-s sound, have the edges of the front teeth touching and the tongue lying on the bottom of the mouth; then blow the air through the teeth.
6. To produce the **sh-h-h** sound, pucker the lips and close the mouth. With the tongue resting on the lower half of the mouth, blow air through the teeth.
7. To **whistle,** pucker the lips, separate the teeth, and blow air through the lips.
8. Other suggested sounds are **eek** (high), **oh** (low) **hum,** and **putt-putt.**

Clapping Sounds

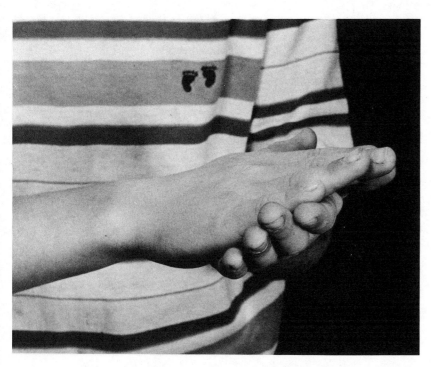

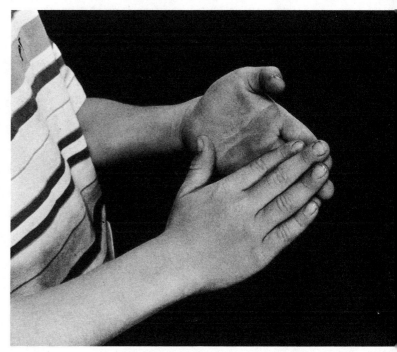

1. Make the basic **clap** rhythm sound by striking the palms of two hands sharply together.

2. The **fingertip clap** rhythm sound is a dull clap made by striking the fingertips of two hands together.

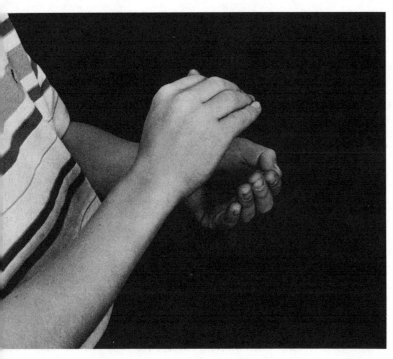 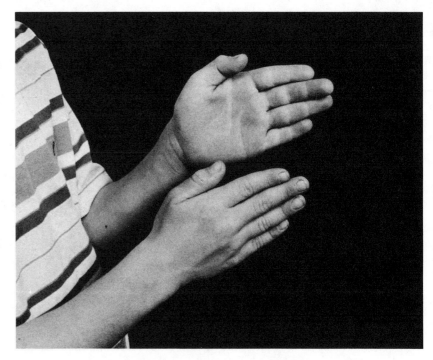

3. The **cup clap** rhythm sound is an echoing sound made by cupping the hands and striking them together.

4. To produce **cymbal clap** rhythm sound raise one hand to chest level in front of the body and place the other at waist level. Move the hands toward each other. As they pass, strike the palms of the hands together to make a clashing sound.

Body Clapping Sounds

1. For the movement called **legs,** clap the sides of the legs with the palms of the hands. Make the **shoulders** sound by clapping the palms of the hands on the shoulders.

2. Slap the palms of the hands on the top of the thighs to produce a sound called **knees.**

Pound Sounds

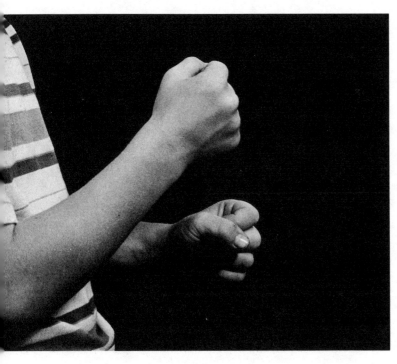
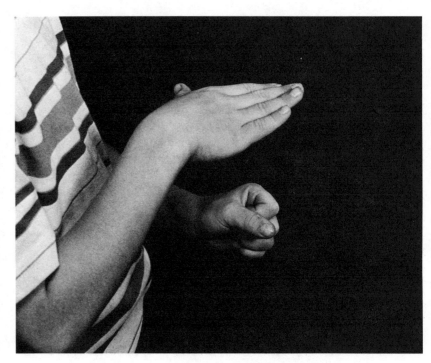

1. Make fists with both hands. Pound one fist on top of the other to make the sound called a **bomb.**

2. A variation is the **clap bomb.** Make a fist with one hand; then clap the fist with the palm of the other hand.

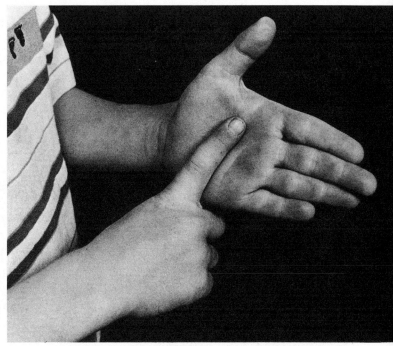

3. Gently hit the legs, arms, or other parts of the body with the fist to produce a sound called the **body bomb.**

4. For the **drum,** extend one hand in front of the body, palm facing up. Slap the open palm with the index finger of the other hand to make a soft drumming noise. By hitting two fingers together, a quieter tapping sound called the **finger drum** can be made.

Brush Sounds

 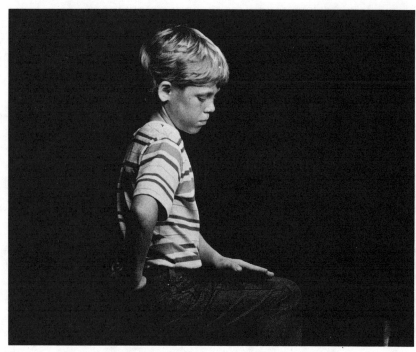

1. For **brush** rhythm sound, slide the palms of the hands back and forth against each other. This should produce a soft rubbing sound.

2. For a **body brush** sound, slide the palm of one hand against a leg or arm. This makes a rubbing sound.

Finger Sounds

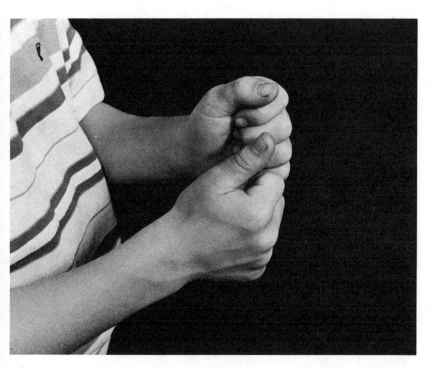

1. For the **knuckle rub,** make a fist with each hand. Rub the knuckles against each other to produce a grating sound.

2. To produce the series of soft tapping sounds called **sequence tapping,** place the palms of the hands together, fingers spread apart. In sequence, tap the little fingers together, then the ring fingers, the middle fingers, and the index fingers.

Snap

Floor Slap

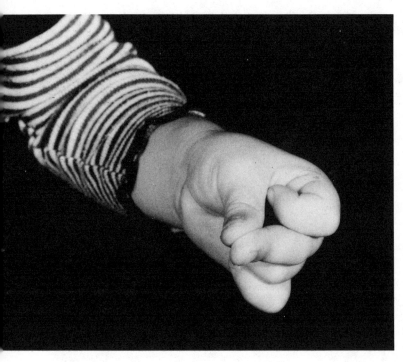

For the **snap** rhythm sound, quickly rub the thumb together with any other finger on the same hand. This should produce a sharp, snapping sound.

Make **floor slap** rhythm sound by slapping the hands on the floor. To reach the floor more easily, bend the knees and lower the body when slapping the floor.

Stomp

1. To produce the **stomp** sound, raise one leg off the ground or floor.

2. Stomp down vigorously to make a loud noise.

Swish

1. For the **swish** sound bend one leg back at the knee, raising the foot off the floor.

2. Move the foot forward, brushing the toe and heel of the foot on the floor.

3. Move the foot forward and off the floor.

4. Brush the heel and then the toe on the floor to complete the swish sound.

Foot Pound Sounds

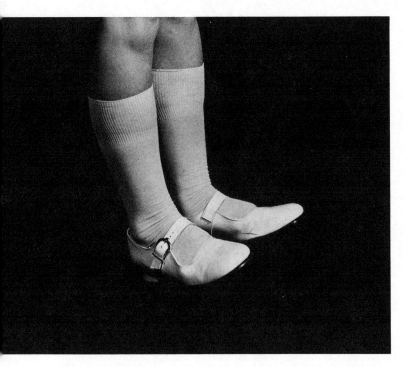 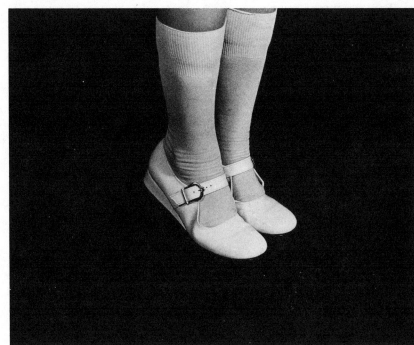

1. Begin the **toes** rhythm sound with both feet flat on the ground. Shift the body weight from the foot to the heels only, and raise the toes off the ground. Bring the toes down forcefully to produce a soft stamping noise.

2. Begin the **heels** rhythm sound with both feet on the ground. Shift the body weight to the toes and raise the heels off the ground. Stomp the heels back down on the ground to produce a thumping noise.

3. A **toe pound** begins with one foot off the ground. Bring the toe of this foot back down forcefully to make a pounding sound.

4. Now tap the heel of this foot on the ground for a **heel pound.**

Step   Hop

 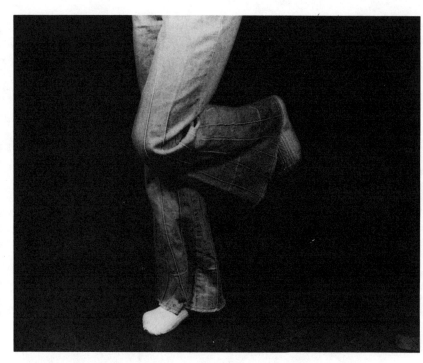

The movement called a **step** is the same movement the foot takes when walking. To begin, lift one foot off the ground. Place this foot gently down on the ground in front of the body to produce a rhythm sound.

For the **hop** movement, lift the foot off the floor by bending the leg backward at the knee. With the foot that is on the ground, make a quick springy leap. The hop movement is complete when the foot returns to the ground.

Jump

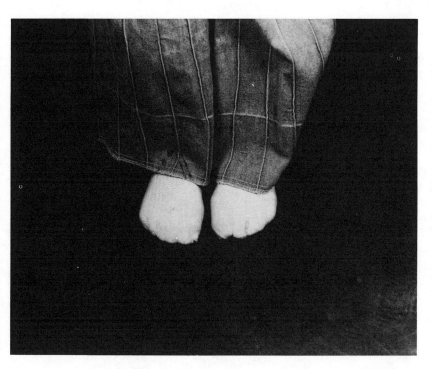

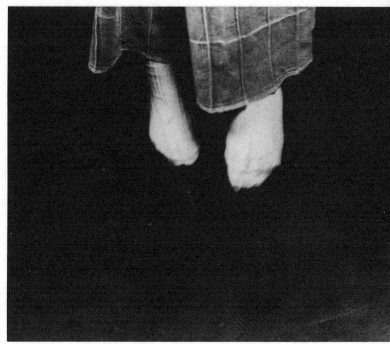

1. Begin the **jump** with both feet on the ground.

2. Using the muscular action of the legs and arms, spring off the ground with both feet. Complete the jump movement by returning both feet to the ground at the same time with a loud noise.

Clapping Sounds with Partners

1. For **clap right,** the partners face each other and clap right hands together. For **clap left,** partners face each other and clap left hands together. The **double clap** is performed with the partners facing each other and clapping both hands together, straight across.

2. For the **cross clap,** partners face each other, arms crossed, and clap right and left hands together at the same time.

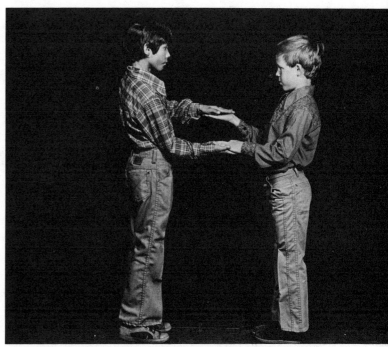

3. Have the partners face each other, one partner with palms up and the other partner with palms down. The partner with palms down slaps his partner's palms for the movement called the **sandwich.**

4. For the **combo sandwich,** each partner has his right palm facing up and his left palm facing down. The partners hit their palms together to produce this rhythm sound.

Exchange Clap

1. Any number of children may perform the **exchange clap** together. Have them sit on their knees, next to each other. Step 1: Each child claps his own knees.

2. The children pick up their hands and clap their right hand on their neighbor's left knee and their left hand on their own right knee at the same time.

3. The children clap their own knees.

4. The children pick up their hands and clap their left hand on their neighbor's right knee and their right hand on their own left knee at the same time.

Step-Together-Step Pattern

1. Begin the **step-together-step** pattern with both feet together; then, with the right foot, step to the right side.

2. Bring the left foot together with the right foot.
3. With the right foot, step to the right side, leaving the feet apart, as in the first photograph. This movement can be repeated, moving from right to left or left to right.

Individual Sound Rhythm Patterns

Pattern 1:
1. Shoulders.
2. Knees.

Pattern 2:
1. Shoulders (hands crossed on chest).
2. Knees.

Pattern 3:
1. Snap.
2. Clap.

Pattern 4:
1. Knees.
2. Clap.
3. Snap.

Pattern 5:
1. Stomp.
2. Snap.
3. Clap.

Pattern 6:
1. Step right.
2. Step together.
3. Step right.
4. Stomp.

Pattern 7:
1–4. Body brush four times.
5. Knees.
6. Clap.
7. Snap right hand.
8. Snap left hand.

Pattern 8:
1. Brush.
2. Brush.
3. Bomb.
4. Bomb.

Pattern 9:
1. Drum.
2. Drum.
3. Cymbal clap.
4. Cymbal clap.

Pattern 10:
1. Heels.
2. Toes.
3. Jump.

Pattern 11:
1. Knuckle rub.
2. Knuckle rub.
3. Cup clap.

Partner Sound Rhythm Pattern

The partners face each other.
1. Knees.
2. Knees.

3. Clap.
4. Clap.

5. Clap right
6. Clap (see step 3–4 photo).

7. Clap left.
8. Clap (see step 3–4 photo).

Body Pass Movements

Shake   Around

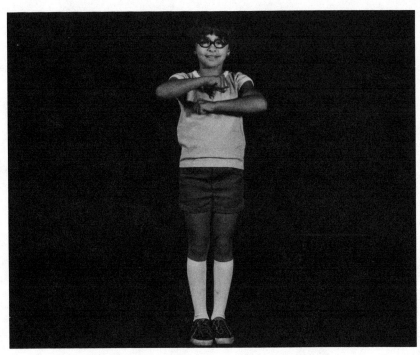

Shake the hands and fingers. The hands can be held at shoulder height with the elbows bent, above the head, or down to the sides of the body.

Bend the arms at the elbows, hands in front of the chest. Place one hand above the other and make a circular pattern with each hand. (The hands may be in a fist or open with the fingers together.)

Hand Movements

1. For the **palm right** pass movement, place the left hand on the hip. Bend the right arm at the elbow and place it in front of the body with palm up.

2. **Palm left** is just the opposite of palm right. The right hand is on the hip; the left arm, bent at the elbow, is placed in front of the body with palm up. For the movement called **palms,** bend both arms at the elbows. Place them in front of the body with palms up.

Body and Head Movements

1. The **bend right** pass movement begins with the hands on the hips and feet spread apart. Bend the body to the right at the waist.

2. Bend the body to the back at the waist for the **bend back** pass movement.

3. Bend the body to the left at the waist for the **bend left** pass movement.

4. Bend the body to the front at the waist for the **bend front** pass movement.
Variation:
   With the head repeat the same movements for the **head right, head back, head left,** and **head front** pass movements. Stand with the feet apart and hands on hips or to the side of the body.

Overhead Arm Movements

1. For the **overhead right** movement, raise the right arm above the head; keep the left hand on the hip. **Overhead left** is the opposite of overhead right. Extend the left arm over the head and place the right hand on the hip.

2. For the **overhead double,** extend both hands above the head.

Arm Circle

 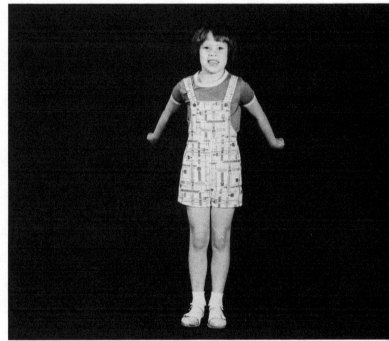

1. The **arm circle** begins with one or both arms out to the side of the body at shoulder height.

2. Move the arms in a circular motion to the sides of the body.

Cross

1. Begin **cross** movement by raising the arms to shoulder height at the side of the body.

2. Bring both arms to the front of the body. The right arm passes over the top of the left arm as the arms reach the middle of the body.

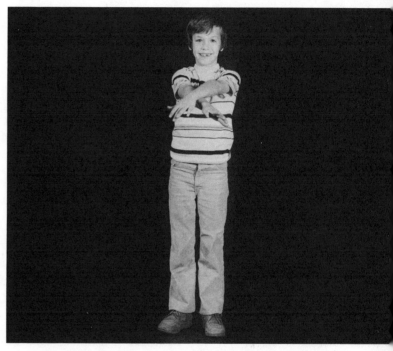

3. Keep the arms extended and move them back to the side of the body.

4. Bring both arms to the middle of the body again. This time pass the left arm over the right arm.

Reach Up and Out Arm Movement

1. Begin the **reach up and out** pass movement sequence with both arms down at the side of the body. Extend both arms over the head.

2. Bend the arms at the elbows and bring the elbows down to the waist while the hands are at shoulder level.

3. Extend the arms out in front of the body at shoulder level.

4. Bend the arms at the elbows and bring the elbows down to the waist while the hands are at shoulder level.

Up Front Arm Movement

1. Begin the **up front** arm movement sequence with the hands on the hips. Stretch the right arm up over the head, keeping it straight. Keep the left hand on the hip.

2. Return the right hand to the hip and extend the left arm over the head.

3. Return the left hand to the hip and extend the right arm in front of the body at shoulder height.

4. Return the right hand to the hip and extend the left arm out in front of the body.

Up 'n' Down Arm Movement

1. The **up 'n' down** pass movement sequence begins with both hands at the side of the body.

2. Raise the arms over the head.

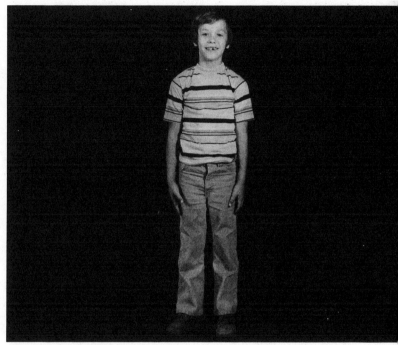

3. Bring the arms to the front of the body to shoulder height.

4. Return the arms to the side of the body.

Zigzag

1. The **zigzag** pass movement begins with arms down at the sides of the body and feet together. Stretch the right hand out from the side of the body at shoulder height, with the fingers together. At the same time, bend the left arm at the elbow and place the hand on the chest.

2. Bend the right arm at the elbow with the hand against the chest while the left hand stretches out to the side of the body.

Step-Toe

1. Begin the **step-toe** movement by stepping forward on the right foot.

2. Then step to the right with the left foot, resting the weight on the toe. To finish the movement, step back on the left foot and bring the right foot back to the left foot, leaving the weight on the toe.

Toe Tap

 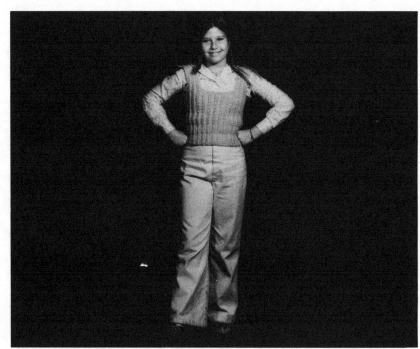

1. Pick the right foot up and place it out to the right side of the body, pointing the toe and tapping it on the ground.

2. Move the right foot to the front of the body, again tapping the pointed toe on the ground.

3. Cross the right foot over the left foot and tap the pointed toe on the ground. This sequence of three movements is called the **toe tap.**

Side Step

1. Begin the **side step** movement with the feet together. With the right foot, step to the side.

2. Return the right foot close against the left foot. This movement can also be done with the left foot stepping to the left side and returning to the right foot.

Rifle

1. The **rifle** pass movement begins with the arms down at the side of the body and the feet together. All at the same time, step backward with the right leg, place the right hand on the waist, and extend the left arm straight out in front of the body.

2. Perform the opposite movement by stepping back on the left leg, placing the left hand at the waist, and extending the right arm in front of the body.

Robot

1. The **robot** pass movement begins with both feet together. Shift the body weight to the left foot. Touch the right toe to the ground in front of the body. Swing the right arm to the back of the body and the left arm forward.

2. With the weight still on the left foot, touch the right toe to the ground behind the body. Swing the right arm forward and the left arm backward. The robot may also be done with the weight on the right foot while the left foot is moved forward and back.

Turn Around

1. The **turn around** movement begins with both feet together. The arms may be down at the side, on the hips, or over the head. With the right foot, step out to the right side.

2. With the left foot step over the right foot, moving the body a quarter turn in a clockwise direction. Continue to turn by repeating these two steps. The turn around pass movement uses four beats to complete the circle and return the body to its starting position.

Rockin'

1. The **rockin'** pass movement begins with the body angling to the right. Bend the knees and swing the arms down.

2. Straighten the legs and pivot on the toes to angle the body to the left. Then bend the knees and swing the arms down. While the arms are swinging the fingers may snap to the beat.

Twist Step

1. Begin the **twist step** with the arms at the side and the feet together. Step forward on the right foot so the entire body faces left. At shoulder height, extend the arms out from the sides of the body (see second photo).

2. Step forward with the left foot so the entire body faces right. Again at shoulder height, extend the arms out from the sides of the body.

Roll Away

1. The **roll away** pass movement begins with both feet together and the hands at the side. Step to the right side with the right foot, keeping the right arm at the side while stretching the left arm above the head.

2. Pivot on the right toe as the left foot steps in front of the right foot to the right. Bring the left arm down to the side of the body while the right arm stretches over the head.

3. Pivot on the left foot as the right foot crosses in front of the left foot to the right. Bring the right arm down to the side of the body and extend the left arm over the head.

4. Pivot on the right foot as the left foot crosses in front of the right foot to the right. Bring the left arm down to the side of the body and extend the right arm over the head.

63

Indian

1. Begin the **Indian** pass movement with both hands at the side of the body. Bring the right arm to shoulder height in front of the body. Touch the fingers of the left hand to the right hand.

2. Keeping the right arm in extended position, touch the right elbow with the left hand.

3. Bend the right arm at the elbow and with the right hand touch the left elbow.

4. The last of this series of four movements is to clap the hands together in front of the body.

Knee Bend

Arm Swing

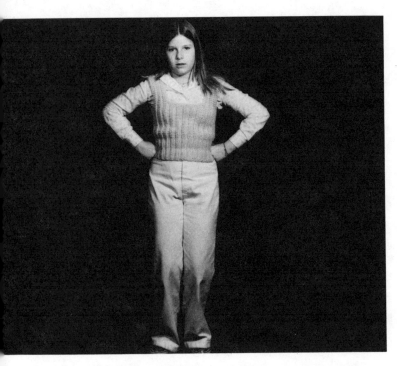

Begin the **knee bend** with both hands on the hips and the feet together. Bend the legs at the knees. Straighten the legs to end the pass movement.

1. Partners face each other and hold hands for the **arm swing.**

2. Swing the hands above the head to one side.

3. Bring the hands down and swing them above the head to the other side.

Shoulder Tap

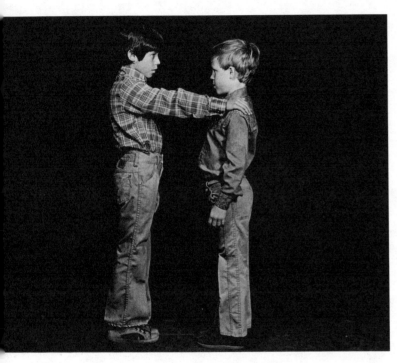

1. The partners face each other for the **shoulder tap.** Each partner taps his right hand on his partner's left shoulder.

2. Complete the movement by having each partner tap his left hand on his partner's right shoulder.

Walking

1. Partners begin with feet together and standing side by side holding hands. They begin with the same foot and step forward together. The partners can walk together in a circle or in a line. The walk does not need to be done with a partner.

2. The partners can also hold hands by joining right hands and left hands together so the arms are crossed.

Step-Kick

1. The partners face each other and hold hands. Each partner steps in place with his right foot while kicking the left foot to the side.

2. The partners then step in place with the left foot while kicking the right foot to the side.

Up and Back Partner Movement

1. The partners face each other and hold hands. Each one steps forward on his right foot as the arms bend at the elbows. The left foot of each partner steps up to the right foot with the weight of the leg on the toe.

2. The partners move away from each other by stepping back on the left foot, stretching the arms out straight and bringing the right foot back next to the left foot with the weight of leg on the toe.

Circle   Bowing

The partners begin by facing each other and joining right and left hands together. The partners may walk in a clockwise or counterclockwise direction.

The partners face each other. The male bows by bending forward at the waist with one hand on his stomach and one hand on his back. The female bows by bending her knees and touching her right toe to the floor behind her left foot, keeping her back straight. She keeps her arms at the side, or holds onto her skirt if she is wearing one.

Hand Turns

1. Partners face each other and place their right palms together.

2. The partners step with the right foot, then the left foot, right foot and left foot, moving in a clockwise circle to complete the turn. This turn is complete in four beats. The turn may also be done by placing left palms together and moving in a counterclockwise circle.

Do-Si-Do

1. The partners begin by facing each other.

2. One partner remains stationary while the other circles him in a clockwise direction. The moving partner walks toward the other partner so their right shoulders are together. He then walks away from the shoulder so he is back to back with his partner.

3. The moving partner walks to the side of his partner so the left shoulders are together. The **do-si-do** is finished when both partners are facing each other again.

Twirl

1. Begin the twirl pass movement with partners facing each other, holding right hands lightly. Raise right arms. One partner stands still while the other goes under her arm and circles in a clockwise direction. When both partners are facing each other again, bring arms down and the twirl is complete.

2. The twirl can also be done with partners holding left hands and one partner circling in a counterclockwise direction.

Mexican Hat Dance Step

1. The partners face each other and join their right and left hands together. The partners jump up together, landing with their left feet flat on the ground and their right feet in front of their bodies, resting on the heels.

2. The partners jump up together again, this time landing with their right feet on the ground and their left feet in front of their bodies, resting on the heels.

Dirty Dishrag

1. The partners face each other and hold hands for the **dirty dishrag** pass movement.

2. The partners swing their arms up to one side. One partner steps forward and under the arms with his right foot; the other partner steps forward and under the arms with his left foot.

3. The partners continue to turn around and under the arms.

4. The step is finished when the partners are facing each other. This movement is completed in four beats.

Individual Body Movement Patterns

Pattern 1:

1. Knees.
2. Knees.

3. Clap.
4. Clap.

5. Around.
6. Around.
7. Around.
8. Around.

Pattern 2:
1. Arms up and clap.
2. Legs.
3. Arms front and clap.
4. Legs.
5. Floor lap.
6. Legs.
7. Arms up and clap.
8. Legs.

Pattern 3:
1. Zigzag right.
2. Zigzag left.
3. Zigzag right.
4. Zigzag left.
5. Arms up.
6. Arms on hips.
7. Arms up.
8. Arms on hips.

Pattern 4:
1. Legs.
2. Right arm to left shoulder.
3. Legs.
4. Left arm to right shoulder.
5. Legs.
6. Both arms crossed to shoulders.
7. Legs.
8. Clap.

Pattern 5:
1. Overhead right.
2. Hands on hips.
3. Overhead left.
4. Hands on hips.
5. Overhead double.
6. Hands on hips.
7. Reach out.
8. Hands on hips.

Pattern 6:
1–16. Step-together-step right four times.
17–32. Step-together-step left four times.
33. Step-toe forward.
34. Step-toe backward.
35. Step-toe forward.
36. Step-toe backward.
37–40. Turn around; clap overhead.

Pattern 7:
1. Palm right.
2. Palm left.
3. Around.
4. Palms.

Pattern 8:
1. Zigzag right.
2. Zigzag left.
3. Rifle.
4. Rifle.
5–8. Arm circle four times.

Pattern 9:

1. Side step right and snap.
2. Step back together and clap.
3. Side step right and snap.
4. Step back together and clap.
5. Side step left and snap.
6. Step back together and clap.
7. Side step left and snap.
8. Step back together and clap.
9. Bend right.
10. Bend left.
11. Bend right.
12. Bend left.

13–16. Up front pass movement.

Partner Body Movement Patterns

Partner Pattern 1:

1–4. Hand turn right.   5–8. Hand turn left.

9–12. Arm swing four times.

13–16. Dirty dishrag.

Partner Pattern 2:
1. Rockin' right (partners standing next to each other).
2. Rockin' left.
3. Rockin' right.
4. Rockin' left.

5–8. Twist forward four times.

9–12. Twist backward four times.

13. Knees (partners facing each other).
14. Clap.
15. Clap right.
16. Clap.
17. Clap left.
18. Clap.
19. Double clap.
20. Clap.

Partner Pattern 3:

1–4. Partners face each other and do-si-do clockwise.

5–8. Join right hands and twirl.

9–12. Up-back.

13–16. Dirty dishrag.

Partner Pattern 4:
1. Partners face each other and shoulder tap right.
2. Shoulder tap left.
3. Shoulder tap right.
4. Shoulder tap left.

5–12. Roll away right.

13–20. Roll away left.

Partner Pattern 5:

1–4. Partners stand side by side holding hands. Walk forward four times.

5–8. Turn and face each other and hold both hands. Step-together-step and stomp back to original position.

9–12. Arm swing four times.

13–16. Circle.

Sticks

Hand Position on Sticks

You will need 2 sticks

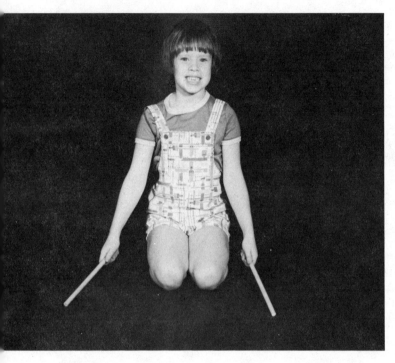

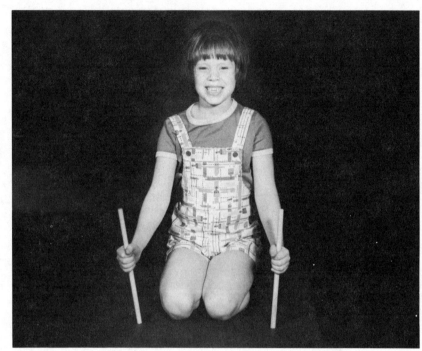

1. The sticks may be held in two ways. The first is to hold the sticks at one end and tap the opposite ends on the floor.

2. The sticks may also be held in the middle and the flat, round ends tapped on the floor.

Hitting Sticks on a Chair

You will need 2 sticks

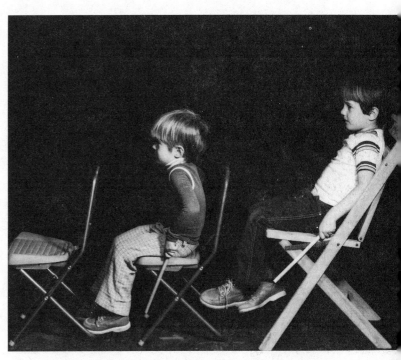

1. Sticks can be used to hit on chairs. Line the chairs up in single file and have the children sit in them. Have the children hold the ends of the sticks and strike them on the back of the chair in front of them. The first chair in the row must be left vacant.

2. The children may also tap their sticks on the sides of their chairs.

Tapping Sticks

You will need 2 sticks

Two sticks can be played by tapping them together.

Partners Tapping Sticks

You will need 2 sticks

1. Partners can hit each other's sticks in several ways, but it works best to select one partner to keep his sticks stationary while the other partner hits them on the outside.

2. Variations are to have one partner keep his sticks stationary while the other partner hits them on the inside or on the tops.

Partner Stick Exchange

You will need 2 sticks

1. Have each partner hold the middle of one stick in his right hand. Hit the bottom of the stick on the floor.

2. Pass the sticks to the partner's left hand. Hold onto the new stick in the left hand.

3. Remove the stick from the left to the right hand and hit it on the ground. The exchange is ready to take place again.

Individual Stick Patterns

Stick Pattern 1:

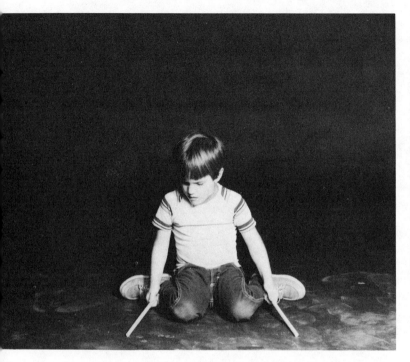

1. Sit on the floor and hold one stick in each hand. Hit the right stick to the right side and the left stick to the left side at the same time.

2. Tap the sticks together at waist level.

3. Tap the sticks together over the head.

Stick Pattern 2:

1–2. Sit down on the floor and hold one stick in each hand. Hit the sticks to the right side two times.

3–4. Hit the sticks to the left side two times.

5–6. Hit the sticks in front of the body on the floor two times.

7. Tap the sticks together at waist level.

8. Tap the sticks together over the head.

Partner Stick Patterns

Partner Stick Pattern 1:

You will need 4 sticks for these patterns

1. Partners face each other, holding one stick in each hand. Hit the sticks to the right side two times.

2. Hit the sticks to the left side two times.

96

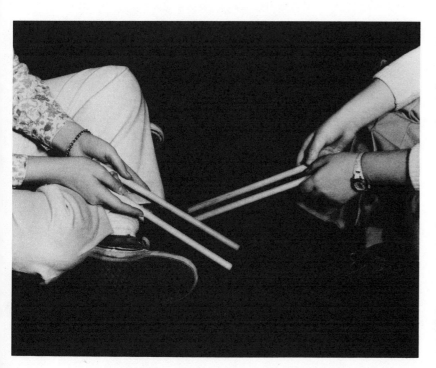

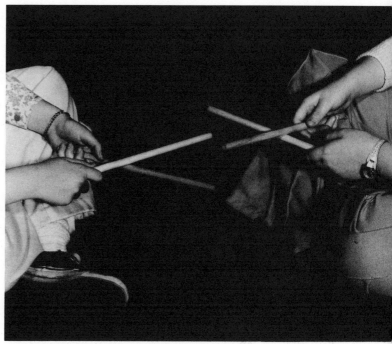

3. Hit the sticks on the floor in front of the body two times.

4. Each partner taps his sticks together at waist level.

 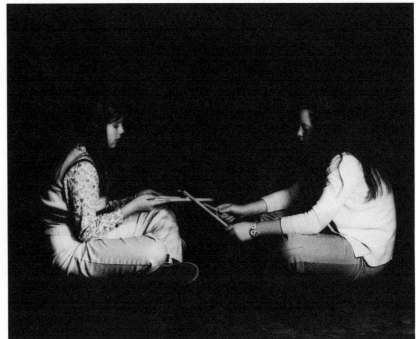

5. One partner keeps his sticks stationary while the other partner hits them on the outside.

7. The same partner hits the outside of the sticks again.

6. The same partner then hits the inside of the stationary partner's sticks.

8. The same partner hits the inside of the sticks.

Partner Stick Pattern 3:

1-2. The partners kneel down next to each other. They have one stick in each hand which they hit to the right side two times.

3-4. Hit the sticks on the floor to the left side two times.

5-6. Hit the sticks on the floor in front two times.

7. Each partner taps his sticks together at waist level.

8. Each partner taps his sticks together over his head.

9-12. Leaning down, each partner walks forward four steps, hitting the sticks on the floor.

13-16. Each partner walks back four steps while he taps his sticks together over his head. On the last step each partner turns to face the other.

17-20. One partner keeps his sticks stationary while the other one hits them on the outside, the inside, the outside, and the inside.

21-24. Each partner taps his sticks together over his head as he turns around.

Partner Stick Pattern 2:

1. The partners sit facing each other and holding the end of a stick in each hand. Hit the sticks on the floor.

2. Each partner hits his sticks together at waist level in front of his body.

3. The partners hit their right sticks together.

4. Each partner hits his sticks together at waist level.

5. The partners hit their left sticks together.

6. Each partner hits his sticks together at waist level.

7. The partners hit both their sticks together.

8. Each partner hits his sticks together at waist level.

Cups

Hitting Cups on the Floor

You will need 2 cups

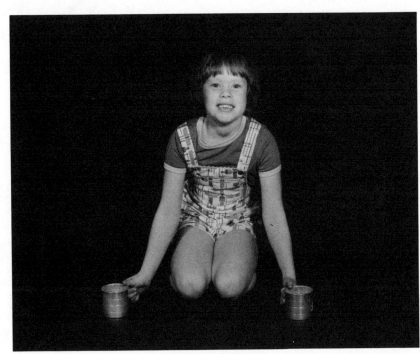

1. Cups can be hit on the floor two different ways. The first is to hit the open ends against the floor.

2. The second way is to hit the bottom of the cups on the floor.

Hitting Cups Together

You will need 2 cups

1. Cups can be tapped against each other with the open ends of the cups.

2. The bottom of the cups may also be hit against each other.

Partner Cup Exchange

You will need 4 cups

1. Have the partners sit facing each other with the cups in front of them. Hit the open ends of the cups on the floor.

2. With his right hand, each partner moves his righthand cup across the floor towards the partner's left hand. With his left hand, each partner slides his lefthand cup to his right hand.

3. Each partner picks up the new cups
   and hits them on the floor. The pattern
   is ready to be repeated.

Individual Cup Patterns

You will need 2 cups for these patterns

Cup pattern 1:
1. Hold one cup in each hand and hit the open ends on the floor to each side of the body.
2. Tap the open ends of the cups together at waist level.
3. Tap the bottom ends of the cups together at waist level.

Cup pattern 2:
1. Hold one cup in each hand and hit the open ends on the floor to each side of the body.
2. Tap the open ends of the cups together over the top of the head.
3. Tap the bottoms of the cups together over the top of the head.

Cup pattern 3:

1–2. Sit on the floor and hold one cup in each hand. Hit the open ends of the cups on the floor to the right side two times.

3–4. Hit the cups on the floor to the left side two times.

5–6. Hit the cups on the floor in front of the body two times.

7. Hit the open ends of the cups together at waist level.

8. Hit the bottoms of the cups together at waist level.

Partner Cup Patterns

Partner Cup Pattern 1:

1. The partners sit facing each other. Each partner has one cup in each hand. Each hits the bottoms of the cups on the ground in front of the body.

2. Each partner hits the open ends of his cups together at waist level.

(Pattern continues on following page)

4. Repeat step 2.

6. Repeat step 2.

8. Repeat step 2.

3. The partners hit the bottoms of their right cups together.

5. The partners hit the bottoms of their left cups together.

7. The partners hit the bottoms of their own cups together.

Partner Cup Pattern 2:
1. The partners sit facing each other with one cup in each hand. Each partner puts one cup to each side of his body and hits the bottoms of the cups on the ground.
2. Each hits the cups on the floor in front of the body.
3. Each hits the cups on the floor with one cup to each side of the body.
4. Each hits the cups on the floor in front of the body.

5–8. Cups exchange two times.

Balls

Bouncing Balls

You will need 1 ball

1. Three different ways of bouncing a ball are used in the following movements. The first is to bounce the ball on the floor with one hand; the second is to bounce the ball using two hands; the third is to alternate the right and left hands.

Variation: The child may do a turn-around, jump, hop, or other movements of the feet while bouncing a ball.

Sweep

You will need 1 ball

1. The ball is held with two hands. Both arms are extended as far to the right side as possible.

2. The arms extend to the left side as far as possible with the ball still in two hands.

Swaying Ball

You will need 1 ball

1. Hold ball in both hands with the arms extended over the head.

2. The arms sway to the right as far as possible with the arms still extended. The arms sway to the left as far as possible.

Angling Ball

You will need 1 ball

1. Hold the ball with two hands and extend the arms out above the right shoulder.

2. Bring the ball down with the arms extended to the side of the left knee. This movement may also be done starting with the ball above the left shoulder and bringing it down to the right knee.

Up and Down Ball Movement

You will need 1 ball

1. Hold the ball with two hands and extend the arms above the head.

2. Keeping the arms extended, move the ball down to waist level.

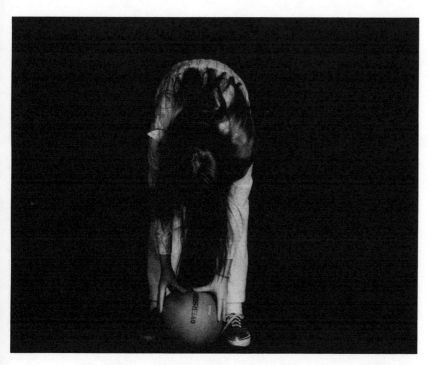

3. Continue to keep the arms extended
   and move the ball down to touch the
   floor. The legs should remain straight
   throughout this sequence of moves.

Ball Circle

You will need 1 ball

1. The **ball circle** consists of four steps. The first step is to hold the ball over the head with two hands.

2. Move the ball to the right side of the body.

118

3. Move the ball below the waist to the front of the body.

Figure eight variation: Hold the ball with two hands, arms extended at waist level. The ball travels above the right shoulder, down below the waist

4. Move the ball up to the left side of the body and back over the head to complete the ball circle.

at the right side, back above the left shoulder, down below the waist at the left side, and returns to starting position.

Bounce Pass

You will need 2 balls

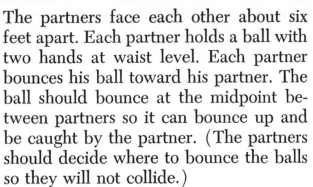

The partners face each other about six feet apart. Each partner holds a ball with two hands at waist level. Each partner bounces his ball toward his partner. The ball should bounce at the midpoint between partners so it can bounce up and be caught by the partner. (The partners should decide where to bounce the balls so they will not collide.)

120

Ball Pass

You will need 2 balls

The partners face each other about six feet apart. Each holds a ball with two hands. The partners throw the ball at each other at the same time. Each one catches the airborne ball before it bounces. (One partner should throw his ball higher than the other so the balls do not collide.)

Individual Ball Patterns

You will need 1 ball for these patterns

Ball Pattern 1:
- 1–4. Bounce the ball four times, exchanging hands.
- 5–8. Ball circle.
- 9. Ball down to the floor.
- 10. Ball up above head.
- 11. Ball down to floor.
- 12. Ball up above head.
- 13–14. Bounce the ball with two hands to the right two times.
- 15–16. Bounce the ball with two hands to the left two times.

Ball Pattern 2:
- 1. Ball angling up right.
- 2. Ball angling down left.
- 3. Ball angling up left.
- 4. Ball angling down right.
- 5. Sweep right.
- 6. Sweep left.
- 7. Sweep right.
- 8. Sweep left.
- 9–12. Bounce ball four times, turning a circle.
- 13–16. Ball circle.

Ball pattern 3:
- 1–4. Hop on right foot and bounce ball four times.
- 5–8. Hop on left foot and bounce ball four times.
- 9–12. Figure eight.
- 13–16. Figure eight.

Partner Ball Patterns

Partner Ball Pattern 1:

1. Partners face each other 6′ apart. Hold the ball in two hands with the arms extended over the head; sway right.
3. Sway right.

2. Sway left.

4. Sway left.

5. Ball up above head.
7. Repeat step 5.

6. Ball down to the floor.
8. Repeat step 6.

9–12. Bounce pass four times.

13–16. Bounce the ball with two hands four times.

Partner Ball Pattern 2:

    1–4. Bounce ball with right hand four times.

    5–8. Bounce ball with left hand four times.

    9–12. Bounce pass four times.

  13–16. Ball pass four times.

Partner Ball Pattern 3:

    1–4. The partners stand side by side and walk four steps forward, bouncing the ball with one hand.

    5–8. Partners walk backward four steps and sweep the ball right, left, right, left. On the last step

    9–12. Jump backward four times, bouncing the ball with two hands.

  13–16. Bounce pass four times.

Partner Ball Pattern 4:

    1–4. The partners face each other about four feet apart, holding the ball with two hands. Ball pass four times.

    5–8. Do-si-do and bounce the ball four times.

    9. Sway right.

  10. Sway left.

  11. Sway right.

  12. Sway left.

  13. Ball up above head.

  14. Ball at waist.

  15. Ball down to floor.

  16. Ball at waist.

Rags

Rag Circle

You will need 1 rag

1. For one version of the rag circle movement, grasp one rag in one hand and make a circle to the side of the body, hitting the rag on the floor. This circle may also be made with one rag in each hand.

2. Another variation uses a rag in each hand, alternating hits on the ground with each rag. For a further variation, extend one arm above the head and make a circle with the rag over the head. A rag circle can also be made with one rag extended in front of the body at shoulder height. Circle with the rag in front of the body, keeping the rag from touching the ground.

Horizontal Rag Up 'n' Down

You will need 1 rag

1. Hold the rag in a horizonal position, one end of the rag in each hand. Raise the arms above the head.

2. Keeping the arms extended, move the rag down to the waist.

Vertical Rag Up 'n' Down

You will need 1 rag

1. Hold a rag in vertical position, one end of the rag in each hand. Raise the top arm as far above the head as possible, and move the other hand as necessary.

2. Pull the rag down as far as possible with the bottom hand, and move the top hand accordingly. Bend from the knees as necessary.

130

Rag Sway

You will need 1 rag

1. Hold the ends of one rag in each hand and extend the arms over the head. Sway the arms to the right.

2. Sway the arms to the left.

Rag Pull

You will need 1 rag

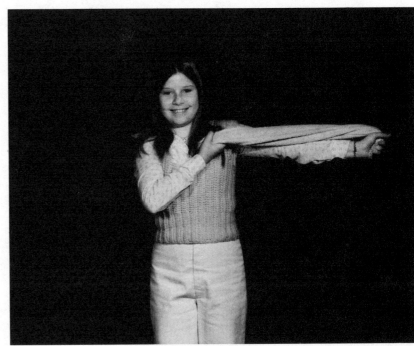

1. Hold the rag at shoulder level and pull it to the right.

2. Pull the rag to the left.

Rag Pull on Angle

You will need 1 rag

1. Hold the ends of one rag in each hand. Raise the right arm above the head to the right side and raise the left arm to the left shoulder. The rag is on an angle.

2. With the left hand, pull the rag down to the level of the left knee and at the same time lower the right hand to the right shoulder. The rag is still on an angle.

Teeter Totter Rags

You will need 1 rag

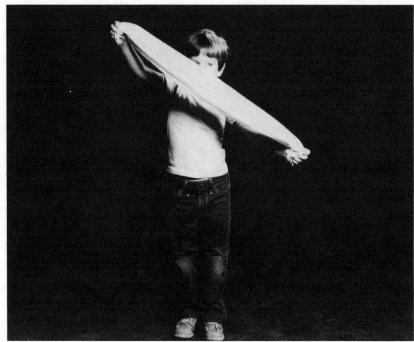

1. Place the ends of one rag in each hand. Extend the arms out at the waist, holding the rag horizontally.

2. Keep the left hand in place and raise the right hand above the head.

3. Bring the right hand down to the waist and raise the left hand above the head.

Lean Back

You will need 2 rags

1. Put one end of each rag in each partner's hands. One partner leans his weight back on his heels. The other partner prevents him from falling by being balanced and holding the rags tightly.

2. The partner who leaned back moves forward and balances while the other partner leans back on his heels.

Rag Pull Forward and Back

You will need 2 rags

1. Have the partners take one end of each rag in their hands. One partner bends his elbows and pulls back on the rags. The other partner follows the move and extends his arms forward to follow the rag.

2. Reverse the action and have the other partner pull back on the rags.

Sawing Rags

You will need 2 rags

Have the partners take one end of each rag in their hands. Each partner pulls his right arm back toward him while the left arms extend to follow the movement. The partners then pull back on their left arms as the right arms extend to follow the movement.

Swinging Rags

You will need 2 rags

Have the partners put one end of each rag in their hands. Swing the arms and rags first to one side and then to the opposite side.

Cross Rags

You will need 2 rags

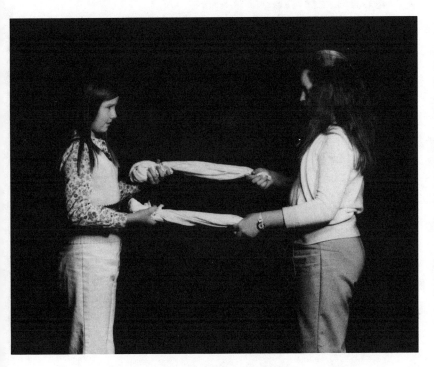 

1. Have the partners hold one end of each rag in their hands. Hold the rags tight at waist level.

2. Have one partner cross his right hand over his left so the rags are crossed. He then crosses his left hand over his right to cross the rags the other way.

Dirty Dishrag with Two Rags

You will need 2 rags

The partners put one end of each rag into their hands. They lift the rags up and over the head and walk under the rags in a clockwise circle. The dirty dishrag movement is finished when both partners again face each other.

Partner Rag Twirl

You will need 1 rag

Each partner takes an end of the one rag in his right hand. They raise the rag up over their heads as each partner walks under the rag and turns in a clockwise circle until he is facing his partner.

Individual Rag Patterns

You will need 1 rag for patterns 1–4; 2 rags for pattern 5

Rag Pattern 1:

1–4. Holding the rag in the right hand, circle the rag to the right side four times.

5–8. Change the rag to the left hand and make a circle to the left side four times.

9. Take one end of the rag in each hand and pull right.

10. Pull left.

11. Pull right.

12. Pull left.

13. Change the rag to a vertical position and pull rag up.

14. Rag down.

15. Rag up.

16. Rag down.

Rag Pattern 2:

1–4. Hold one end of the rag in each hand. Teeter totter four times.

5. Rag horizontal, up.

6. Rag horizontal, down.

7. Pull right.

8. Pull left.

Rag Pattern 3:

1. Hold one end of the rag in each hand. Sway right.

2. Sway left.

3. Sway right.

4. Sway left.

5–8. Circle rag over head four times.

9–16. Repeat entire pattern, steps 1–8.

Rag Pattern 4:
1. Hold the rag horizontally, one end of the rag in each hand.
2. Rag down.
3. Rag up.
4. Rag down.
5. Angle up.
6. Angle down.
7. Angle up.
8. Angle down.
9. Sway right.
10. Sway left.
11. Sway right.
12. Sway left.
13. Rag up.
14. Rag waist.
15. Rag up.
16. Rag waist.

Rag Pattern 5:
1–4. Hold one rag in each hand. Circle rags, alternating hits on the floor.
5–8. Circle rags over head.
9–12. Circle rags to the sides.
13–16. Circle rags in front of the body.

Partner Rag Patterns

You will need 2 rags for these patterns

1–4. Partners hold the end of one rag in right hand and circle four times.

5–8. Change the rags to the left hand and circle four times.
(Pattern continues on next page)

143

9. Each partner puts an end of his rag in each hand and sways right.

11. Sway right.

10. Sway left.

12. Sway left.

13. Horizontal rags up.
15. Repeat step 13.

14. Horizontal rags down.
16. Repeat step 14.
    (Pattern continues on next page)

17–20. Partners grasp ends of each other's rags and saw rags four times.

21–22. Drop the end of the rag in the left hand and circle with the rag in the right hand two times. (See photo for steps 1–4.)

23–24. Change the rag to the left hand and circle two times. (See photo for steps 5–8.)

146

Partner Pattern 2:

1–4. Partners face each other with an end of the two rags in each hand. Rag swing four times.

5–6. One partner crosses his right hand over his left.

7–8. Same partner crosses left hand over right.

9. First partner leans back.

10. Second partner leans back.

11. First partner leans back.

12. Second partner leans back.

13–16. Dirty dishrag.

Partner Pattern 3:

1–4. One partner does a do-si-do around the other as both teeter totter with their rags until the movement is finished.

5–8. The other partner does a do-si-do around the first partner as both teeter totter with their rags.

9–12. Rag pull forward and back four times.

13–16. Dirty dishrag.

Hoops

Hoop on the Floor

You will need 1 hoop

1. Lay the hoop on the floor. The children jump or hop into the hoop.

2. The children then jump out of the hoop.

3. The children walk, skip, jump, hop, or run around the hoop.

Variation:

Put two rows of hoops together in a long line on the floor. The children jump, walk, or hop from hoop to hoop, making up a pattern as they move.

Hoop Jumping

You will need 1 hoop

Place both hands on the hoop about twelve inches apart from each other. Raise the hoop over the head, bring it down in front of the body, and jump over the bottom edge of the hoop.

Hoop Turn

You will need 1 hoop

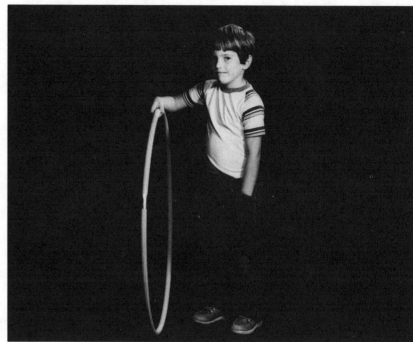

Hold the hoop with one hand and stand it on one edge on the floor. Walk to the right in a clockwise circle; the hoop turns to follow the clockwise circle. Continue walking clockwise until the circle is finished.

Up 'n' Down Hoop Movement

You will need 1 hoop

1. Hold the hoop with two hands and extend it over the head.

2. Bring the hoop down to the waist level; then bring the hoop down to touch the floor.

Hoop Circle

You will need 1 hoop

1. Hold the hoop with two hands on the sides of the hoop. Extend the arms and hoop over the head.

2. Circle down to the right side.

152

3. Continue to circle down so the hoop touches the floor.

4. Circle up to the left side and return the hoop over the head.

Rockin' Hoop

You will need 1 hoop

1. Put one edge of the hoop on the floor and one hand on each side of the hoop. Bend the right knee and rock the hoop and the body to the right.

2. Straighten up the body; then bend the left knee and rock the hoop and body to the left.

Swaying Hoop

You will need 1 hoop

1. Hold onto the hoop with two hands and extend it over the head. Sway the arms and hoop to the right.

2. Sway the hoop and arms to the left.

Steering Wheel

You will need 1 hoop

1. Place one hand on each side of the hoop and hold the arms at shoulder level in front of the body.

2. Turn the hoop like a steering wheel to the right. The left hand will be on top of the hoop and the right one on the bottom.

3. Turn the hoop to the left so the right hand will be on the top of the hoop and the left hand will be on the bottom.

Have one or two children hold a hoop while another child walks through it.

Hoop Pull

You will need 1 hoop

1. Place one hand on each side of the hoop and extend the arms at shoulder level. Pull the hoop to the right so the right arm is straight and the left arm is bent at the elbow.

2. Pull the hoop to the left so the left arm is straight and the right arm is bent at the elbow.

Dirty Dishrag with Hoop

You will need 1 hoop

Have the partners hold onto the hoop and raise it above their heads. Walk under the hoop and turn a clockwise circle. Hold the hoop loosely so the hands can slip around it.

Hoop Toss

You will need 1 hoop

Have the partners face each other about six feet apart. Have one partner toss the hoop in the air. The other partner catches the hoop with one or two hands.

Partner Hoop Exchange

You will need 2 hoops

1. Each partner holds one hoop at his side in his right hand.

2. Bring the hoop up to the waist and take the partner's hoop in the left hand. At the same time, let go of the hoop in the right hand.

3. Place the hoop down at the left side.

4. Raise the hoop again and repeat the hoop exchange.

Individual Hoop Patterns

You will need 1 hoop for these patterns

Hoop Pattern 1:
1. Steering wheel right.
2. Steering wheel left.
3. Steering wheel right.
4. Steering wheel left.
5–8. Circle.

Hoop Pattern 2:
1. Hoop up.
2. Hoop waist.
3. Hoop down.
4. Hoop waist.
5. Pull right.
6. Pull left.
7. Pull right.
8. Pull left.
9. Lay hoop on ground and jump in.
10. Jump out.
11. Jump in.
12. Jump out.
13–16. Walk around hoop.

Hoop Pattern 3:
1. Pull hoop right.
2. Pull hoop left.
3. Pull hoop right.
4. Pull hoop left.
5. Hoop up.
6. Hoop down to the floor.
7. Hoop up.
8. Hoop down to the floor.

Hoop Pattern 4:
1–4. Hoop jumping, four times.
5. Sway right.
6. Sway left.
7. Sway right.
8. Sway left.
9. Rockin' hoop right.
10. Rockin' hoop left.
11. Rockin' hoop right.
12. Rockin' hoop left.
13–16. Hoop turn.

Partner Hoop Patterns

You will need 1 hoop for Partner Hoop Pattern 1; 2 hoops for patterns 2 and 3

Partner Hoop Pattern 1:

1–4. The partners face each other. One partner holds the hoop with both hands. The other partner walks through and circles the hoop.

5–8. The partner who has just finished walking through and circling the hoop then holds the hoop while the other partner walks through the hoop and circles it.

9–12. Dirty dishrag.

13–16. Hoop toss four times.

Partner Hoop Pattern 2:

1. Partners face each other. Sway right.
2. Sway left.
3. Sway right.
4. Sway left.

5–6. Exchange hoops.

7–8. Exchange hoops.

9. Rockin' hoop right.
10. Rockin' hoop left.
11. Rockin' hoop right.
12. Rockin' hoop left.

13–16. Turn around.

Partner Hoop Pattern 3:

1. Partners stand side by side 3' apart, each holding one hoop. Hoop up.
2. Hoop down to the floor.
3. Hoop up.
4. Hoop down to floor.

5–8. Hoop circle

9. Pull right.
10. Pull left.
11. Pull right.
12. Pull left.

13–16. Turn around.

Ropes

Jump Rope with One

You will need 1 6′ rope

Hold an end of the rope in each hand.
Start the rope behind the feet, turn the
hands in counterclockwise circles, and
jump over the rope as it hits the ground.

Jump Rope with Three or More

You will need 2 10' ropes

1. The first and easiest kind of jump rope is called Blue Bells. Two children sway the rope from side to side and a child jumps the rope as it hits the ground in the middle. Two children can also move their hands together to turn the rope in a clockwise circle. The child who jumps may stand next to the rope as it is started, or he may run into the rope after it has hit the ground.

2. In Double Dutch, the most difficult method, the children turn two ropes at once, one of them clockwise and the other counterclockwise. As the ropes hit the ground alternately, the child jumps from side to side. The child must learn how to run into the turning ropes because it is difficult to start the two ropes when a child is next to them.

Walking on the Ropes

You will need 1 10′ rope

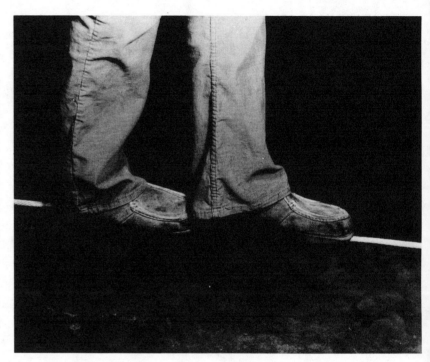

1. Use a regular **walking** movement on the rope with the feet apart and move forward or backward.

2. Walk on the rope in **heel-toe** fashion. After the first step (a regular walking step), the heel of the foot is placed touching the toe of the other foot. Continue to walk forward or backward in this fashion.

Besides turning ropes, ropes can be laid flat on the ground in straight lines to walk on. Use the specific steps on this page and the following pages, or adapt patterns from the previous sections to add the thrill of balance.

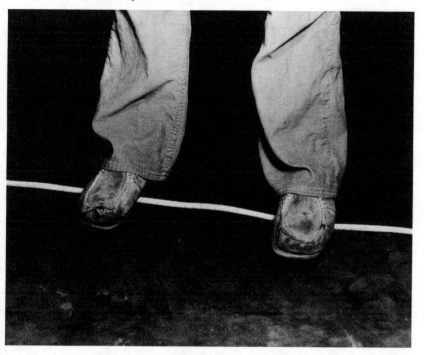 

3. For the **sideways walk,** step with the right foot first, then bring the left foot to the right foot and step again with the right foot.

4. The **sideways cross walk** is executed by crossing the left foot over the right foot. The right foot swings in back of the left foot and steps right.

Scissor Walk

You will need 1 10′ rope

 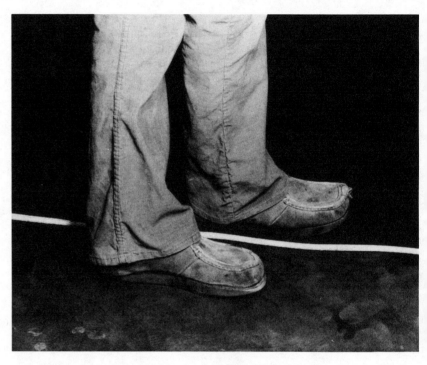

1. Begin the **scissor walk** with the right foot stepping to the left side of the rope. The left foot crosses over the right foot and over the rope without touching it, and steps to the right side of the rope.

2. Take the right foot from behind the left foot, cross in front of it over the rope, and step to the left side of the rope.

Jump Turns

You will need 1 10' rope

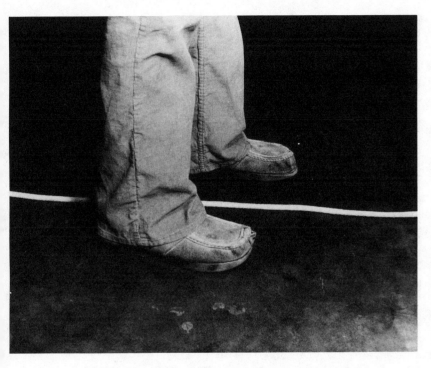 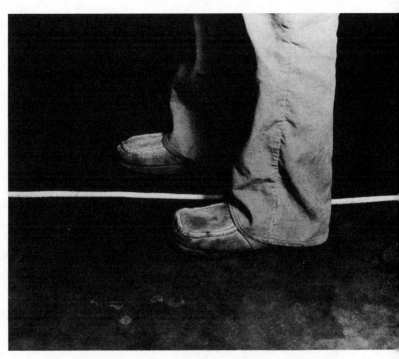

1. Lay a rope flat on the ground. Jump over the rope with the right foot on the right side of the rope and the left foot on the left side of the rope.

2. Jump up with both feet, turning in the air at the same time, and land facing in the opposite way to the direction the jump began.

Jumping Over Ropes

You will need 1 10′ rope

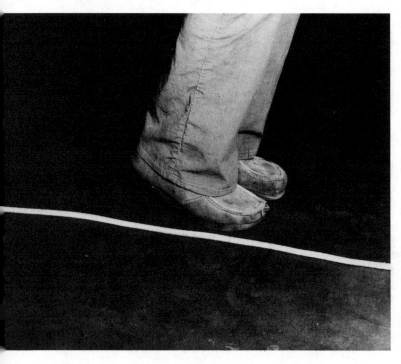

1. Lay a rope flat on the ground. Stand on the left side of the rope and jump to the right side of the rope.

2. From the right side of the rope, jump forward and over the rope to the left side. Do not touch the rope.

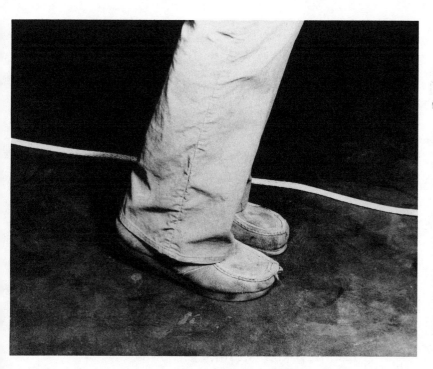

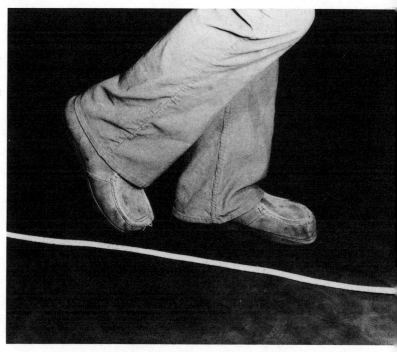

3. From the left side, jump again, forward and to the right side, continuing toward the far end of the rope. This is called **alternate jumping.**

4. **Alternate hopping** uses the same pattern as alternate jumping except by hopping on one foot over the rope.

Individual Rope Patterns

*You will need 1 10′ rope for patterns 1 and 2;
1 16′ rope or 2 8′ ropes for patterns 3 and 4*

Rope Pattern 1:
- 1–4. Lay the rope in a straight line on the floor. Scissor walk forward four times.
- 5–8. Walk sideways four times.
- 9–12. Heel-toe walk backward four times.
- 13–16. Step-kick forward four times.

Rope Pattern 2:
- 1–2. Jump turn two times.
- 3–6. Alternate jumping four times.
- 7–8. Jump turn two times.
- 9–12. Alternate hopping four times.
- 13–16. Scissor walk.

Rope Pattern 3:
- 1–4. Outline a 4′ x 4′ square with the rope. Begin on one side of the square and walk forward four times.
- 5–8. Turn the corner on the rope. Walk backward four times.
- 9–12. Turn the corner on the rope. Alternate jump four times.
- 13–16. Turn the corner on the rope. Heel-toe walk four times.

Rope Pattern 4:
- 1–4. Make a circle with the rope. Step-together-step-together.
- 5–8. Sideways cross walk.
- 9–12. Step-kick-step-kick.
- 13–16. Jump turn four times.

Index of Sounds and Movements

175